For Laurie
A wonderful maker of things

My thanks to Jazzy Laurie Tom Sarah Stevie
Ollie Rufus Ben Jill

Copyright © 2012 by Lucy Cousins

Maisy™. Maisy is a registered trademark of Walker Books Ltd, London.

First U.S. edition 2012

Library of Congress Cataloging-in-Publication Data is available.

Library of Congress Catalog Card Number pending

ISBN 978-0-7636-6122-9

12 13 14 15 16 17 TLF 10 9 8 7 6 5 4 3 2 1

Printed in Dongguan, Guangdong, China

This book was typeset in Gill Sans MT.
The illustrations were done in gouache.

Candlewick Press
99 Dover Street
Somerville, Massachusetts 02144

visit us at www.candlewick.com

Create with Maisy

by Lucy Cousins

CANDLEWICK PRESS

A Message for the Grown-ups

Making things is fun.

In this book, Maisy makes a lot of things that I hope you and your children will enjoy making too. The instructions are very simple, and you don't need to follow them if you have your own ideas. I hope that you will already have most of the things needed in your home, but if not, just use something different.

While your children are enjoying making things, please make sure they are safe. Help them where necessary and always use:

• glue and glue sticks that are washable and nontoxic

• child-friendly scissors with rounded ends

• washable nontoxic paints, like poster paints

Any birthdays coming up? I think homemade gifts are the best presents. I still cherish things my teenage children made for me when they were little.

Have fun!

Love,

Lucy Cousins

Maisy loves making things.

These are some of the things she uses.

You can make things too.

Beady Butterfly

flitter

flutter

Maisy uses:

cardboard

scissors

paints and brushes

pipe cleaners

beads

tape

How to Make It

1. Cut a butterfly body from the cardboard, and paint it.

2. To make the wings, thread some beads onto two pipe cleaners.

3. Bend the pipe cleaners into wing shapes. Twist the ends, and tape them to the back of the body.

4. For the antennae, bend a pipe cleaner in half and tape it to the butterfly's head.

5. Thread two eye beads onto the antennae, and curl the ends.

Box House

Maisy uses:

a cardboard box

a pen or pencil

cardboard

scissors

tape

paints and brushes

Maisy has made a house for Panda too.

How to Make It

1. Draw a door on the box.

2. Get a grown-up to help you cut out the door. Leave one of the long sides uncut so that the door can swing open.

3. To make the roof, fold a piece of cardboard lengthwise. Attach the roof to the top of the house with tape.

4. Add a cardboard chimney, then paint and decorate your house!

Blossom Tree

Maisy uses:

a large piece of cardboard

paints and brushes

a drinking straw

tissue paper

a glue stick

How to Make It

1. On the cardboard, paint a large tree with four branches.

2. Add water to the paint, and brush some paint drops onto the branches.

3. Using the straw, blow the paint in different directions—making lots of little branches.

4. Tear the tissue paper into small pieces, and scrunch them into balls to form blossoms.

5. When the painted tree is dry, glue on the tissue blossoms.

cheep cheep

Food
Garden

Maisy uses:

paper

glue and brush

Seeds, dried herbs, spices, beans, and pasta

How to Make It

1. Use the brush and glue to paint a flower on a sheet of paper. Sprinkle some seeds, herbs, or other similar items on top of the glue.

2. Gently shake off the loose seeds or herbs.

3. Follow this process to create petals, stems, and leaves until you have a beautiful garden!

Vegetable Print

Maisy uses:

fruit and vegetables

paper towels

paper plates

paints

paper

How to Make It

1. Ask a grown-up to help you cut up some fruit and vegetables. Pat the slices dry with a paper towel.

2. Spread paint onto paper plates.

3. Dip the sliced fruit or vegetables into the paint, and print patterns on the paper.

Maisy uses her prints as Wrapping paper.

Pencil Holder

maisy
uses pictures
of her
favorite animals.

Maisy uses:

a plastic container from her recycling bin

glue and a brush

pictures cut out from magazines

ribbon

stickers

How to Make It

1. Find a plastic container.

2. Use the glue and brush to stick on pictures and ribbon.

3. Add stickers or any other decorations you like.

Maisy keeps pencils and crayons in her container.

Painted Pebbles

Maisy uses:

pebbles

paints and brushes

How to Make Them

1. Find some smooth pebbles that are nice shapes and colors.

2. Paint them with bright pictures and patterns.

Feathery Mask

Maisy uses:

a paper plate

scissors

paints and brushes

feathers

tape

a Popsicle stick

Is that you, Cyril?

How to Make It

1. Hold the plate to your face, and ask a grown-up to draw eye holes.

2. Ask the grown-up to help you cut out the eye holes.

3. Paint a colorful face on the plate.

4. Use tape to attach feathers to the back.

5. For a handle, tape the Popsicle stick to the bottom of the mask.

Paper Lanterns

Maisy uses:

colored paper

paints and brushes

scissors

tape

ribbon or string

How to Make Them

1. Cut some rectangles out
of paper, and paint
patterns on them.
Leave them to dry.

2. Fold the paper
in half lengthwise.

3. Make a row of
cuts along the
folded edge.

4. Unfold the paper.
Roll it so the short
ends meet. Join
with tape.

5. For a handle, cut a strip of paper,
and tape it onto
the lantern.

6. Make more lanterns.

7. Thread ribbon or string through
the handles, and hang them up.

Maisy is going
to have a
party.

Tissue Flowers

buzzzzz

Maisy makes flowers for Ella.

Maisy uses:

tissue paper

scissors

pipe cleaners

beads

How to Make Them

1. To make one flower, hold together several layers of tissue paper and roughly cut a circle.

2. Pierce the center of the tissue circles with a pipe cleaner. Then thread a bead onto the tip of the pipe cleaner.

3. Bend the pipe cleaner around the bead and twist.

4. Scrunch up the tissue circles, then separate the petals.

5. Make more flowers. If you want to make them sparkly, dab them with glue and add glitter.

Vegetable Characters

Maisy uses:

fruit and vegetables

a cutting board and knife

toothpicks

How to Make Them

1. Choose a fruit or vegetable for your character's body. Then choose other items for its legs, face, and other details.

2. Ask a grown-up to help if you need to cut things up.

3. Use the toothpicks to join things. To connect small pieces, you may want to snap a toothpick in half.

Hello, Zucchini Dog.

Charlie likes Mr. Eggplant.

Button Bowl

Maisy uses:

air-dry clay (which can be bought online or from a craft store)

buttons, beads, sequins, shells, and glitter

How to Make It

1. Squeeze the clay in your hands and make a ball.

2. Press your thumbs into the middle, and use your fingers to shape a bowl.

3. Flatten out the bottom to make a base.

4. Press buttons and other decorations into the clay.

5. Leave the bowl to dry for about 24 hours.

Panda loves the button bowl.

Pasta Necklace

Maisy uses:

dry pasta tubes

brushes and paints

string

scissors

glue

sequins

How to Make It

1. Paint some pasta tubes in different colors, and leave them to dry.

2. Thread the pasta onto a piece of string.

3. Check to be sure the necklace will fit over your head.

4. Tie a knot in the string.

5. Glue on sequins for extra sparkle.

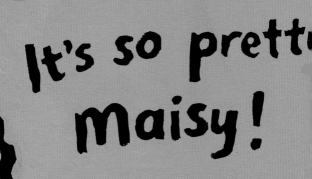

It's so pretty, Maisy!

twinkly

sparkly

shiny

lovely

Sparkly Crown

Maisy uses:

colored paper

shiny wrappers,
foil, and stickers

a glue stick

tape

How to Make It

1. Wrap the paper around your head and cut it to size.

2. Unroll the paper and cut a zigzag around the top.

3. Using a glue stick, attach shiny wrappers, bits of foil, and stickers to your crown.

4. Join the ends with tape.

Hello, King Eddie!

Magic Wax Painting

Maisy uses:

white paper

white wax crayon

paints and brushes

How to Make It

1. Draw a picture with the wax crayon.

2. Brush watery paint all over the paper, especially near the wax lines. Watch your picture appear!

Rainbow Tiger

Maisy uses:

cardboard

lots of things from her recycling bin

glue

How to Make It

1. Cut the tiger's body from cardboard.

2. Create the rest of the tiger using recycled things. Try forks for legs, buttons for eyes, and cut-up magazines for stripes.

3. Glue all the pieces onto a cardboard backing.

Colorful Cookies

Maisy uses:

sugar cookies

powdered sugar

a bowl and some spoons

sprinkles, candy, and fruit

writing icing

How to Make Them

1. Wash your hands.

2. Put 4 heaped tablespoons of powdered sugar into a bow

3. Add 3–4 teaspoons of water and stir.

4. Spread the icing on the cookies, and leave them to dry a little.

5. Decorate the iced cookies with sprinkles, candy, fruit, and writing icin

Yummy!

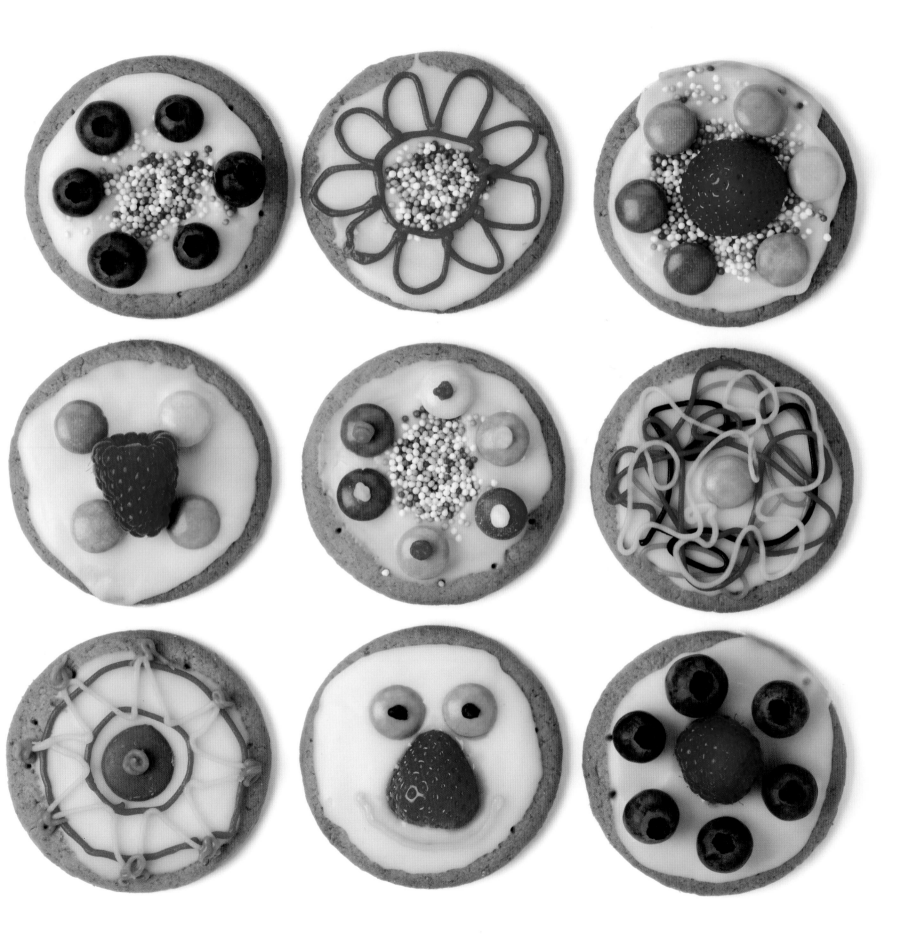

Maisy has been very busy.
She has made lots of things.

Nice work, Maisy!

To Maddison Jane, who inspired this book
— J. Y.

To Jack Andrew and Peter with much love
and to Ginger and Maria
— L. M.

First Edition

Library of Congress Cataloging-in-Publication Data

Yolen, Jane.
Off we go! / by Jane Yolen ; illustrated by Laurel Molk.
p.   cm.
Summary: One by one, baby woodland creatures leave home and sing their way to visit grandma.
ISBN 0-316-90228-4
[1. Animals—Infancy—Fiction. 2. Grandmothers—Fiction. 3. Stories in rhyme.]
I. Molk, Laurel, ill. II. Title.
PZ8.3.Y760f 1999
[E]—dc21   98-6893

10 9 8 7 6 5 4 3 2

TWP

Printed in Singapore

The illustrations for this book were done in watercolor on 140 lb. hot press Arches paper.
The text was set in Cochin, and the display type was hand-lettered by Judythe Sieck.